Linchpins by Ellie Rose McKee
www.ellierosemckee.com

Copyright © 2021 Ellie Rose McKee

All rights reserved.

This book or any portion thereof may not be reproduced or used in any manner whatsoever without the express written permission of the publisher except for the use of brief quotations in a book review.

ISBN: 978-1-8384323-1-7

Linchpins

Poems

WWW.ELOWENPRESS.COM

Contents

1. Breathe — Page 1
2. An Ode to Pockets — Page 2
3. Clock Watching — Page 3
4. Women's Issues — Page 4
5. Birdsong — Page 5
6. Cat in the Window — Page 6
7. Fish Out of Water — Page 7
8. X/Y — Page 8
9. What I Think About When I Can't Sleep — Page 9
10. Mother Russia — Page 10
11. Linchpins — Page 11
12. Benji — Page 12
13. Beards — Page 13
14. A Lesson in Etymology — Page 15
15. Homeland — Page 16
16. Fragile — Page 18
17. Wonder/To Look Up — Page 19
18. Bank Holiday Blues — Page 20
19. Bolt — Page 21
20. Diagnoses — Page 22
21. Stream of… — Page 23
22. The Cost of Words — Page 24
23. Fault Lines — Page 25
24. Rubatosis — Page 26
25. Paper Hands — Page 27

Acknowledgements — Page 28

Linchpins

Ellie Rose McKee

Breathe

The tiny, deafening breath
must ring out and reach the sky
before the laboured breath of mother earth
can return

to normal. This is how it must be–
how it will always be, from now on–
the very definition of normal
changed in a cry.

Linchpins

An Ode to Pockets

I stand at the bus stop and try
not to think about my last
appointment. Go to bury
my hands in my pockets

        but of course, there are none.

No pockets, fake pockets,
pockets that could only hold a tissue–
and only just. The difference between
a good dress and a great dress
        is pockets.

Pockets are proof of forethought.
Evidence the designer 'got it'
or cared.

I'm almost fooled into thinking
that pockets are not generally cared
about, but they would never be left
out of a man's garment.

Indeed, the men often get extra.
Maybe that's where all the women's pockets go.
Or maybe…

maybe the pockets men have–
that are twice the size and double
in number–are an intended insult to us;
are meant to rub in the fact that

women are expected to carry so much.

Clock Watching

Minutes and hours go by;
I sit and watch them pass–
vanish into the night.

Distracted, my eyes
    slip
from the clock
and close.

Opening again, they see
the seconds have
slipped some more.

My vigilance (it seems)
is all for naught.

When I move on,

ticking hands
        will
                not
stutter.

Linchpins

Women's Issues

Did you ever notice the absence of signs
for 'feminine care' products at the store?
The capitalists like to pretend
they don't exist. It's unseemly to be
a woman, much less care about yourself.
Less than that: have needs all your own.

Period pads are in the baby isle, shoved
off to the side with all the other
woman stuff. No one thinks
about those women trying desperately
to conceive and how hard
it is for them to walk past formula
and baby bibs and a thousand other
things designed for tiny hands

we may never touch.
Marketing officers do not consider me.
Chief executives in office blocks
think it fine to call the clinic an infertility
clinic because that's what it is, isn't it? No.
Speaking from experience, no.
The words matter. It's a *fertility* clinic and it's hard

enough to walk in there without that sign hanging
above your head on top of everything else.
Nurses, a word: don't tell someone their baby has no

heartbeat in a room beside the labour ward. Tears
of joy and grief should never be mixed. Screams
of pain and screams of agony have different strains.

Do not let them contaminate the same air.

Ellie Rose McKee

Birdsong
for WomenXBorders

Bright as shining pins,
we paraded through the Dublin streets;

Pins working double time
to keep up with the rest of the flock.

Then, at the roost, we gathered;
more of us – a murmuration.

Silence fell, we opened our beaks,
and sang.

Linchpins

Cat in the Window

How much
do you think she understands?

Does she see her place in the world?
In our lives?

We are her second set of humans.
She is your third ever cat.

My second feline.
Twenty-second pet.

Our cat—our current cat—only
cat we've ever owned, knows nothing

of Tess and Scruff and Benji and Scamp.
Of the paw prints pressed into our hearts

that she steps
                into each
                                new day.

She yawns and pushes through the blinds,
now hidden from my gaze, her profile a shadow.

Sox turns her face to the window
and watches the empty street.

Ellie Rose McKee

Fish Out of Water

Adrenaline, adventure, air
Nothing it could live on
But surely everything it lived *for*

Leaping from that lake
The fish surely gasped for breath

And was left wanting

Surely it felt the water drip off its gills
As it felt the sunshine upon its scales
And surely it felt great in that moment

An addictive small sense of panic
Before plunging back into those depths

X/Y

The laws of attraction:
an opposing force?

Always the first to raise my hand in Bible study,
I thought questioning natural.

Too long, it took, to puzzle out.

Natural and normal weren't always the same.
Not everyone had those feelings.

For some,
there was nothing to deny.

Ellie Rose McKee

What I Think About When I Can't Sleep

Gently cracking ice

the pond, out back
slowly melting

Creaking stairs and floorboards
in the old house
as it settles, for the night

and the heat from the dying fire

The tiny sigh
of a dog in its sleep

A wonderful host of sounds
that too often go

        Unnoticed
        Unheard
        Unloved

Linchpins

Mother Russia

A doll within
the arms of a tot
within the arms
of her mother,
her mother's mother.

Generations nesting.
Empty nests.

Emptiness.

Ellie Rose McKee

Linchpins

Swiss army wife—
no cape, no mask,
only tasks
(maybe an apron).

Unpaid,
like all good superheroes.
Multi-purpose,
like those scissors in that drawer.

You know the drawer for
all the things you could ever need
that don't quite   *fit*
anywhere else?

> String,
> shoelaces,
> sleep,
> and such.

Those scissors, stuffed
far away in the back, are dull
from years of duty—cutting
time, food, corners;
hair, clothes, and card.

The universe would self-destruct
if the pin ever managed to pull loose, but

how long before
anyone would notice?

Linchpins

Benji

I never talk about you anymore,
and am shamed by my lack of grief.

Maybe the years have dulled it.
Maybe I packed up that hurt
and it's dusty but still intact–
out of sight, out

of mind. It seems
your absence now
is as unobtrusive as your
presence used to be.

So perhaps, then, it's fitting.
Perhaps treading gently from
the life of a troubled child
to somewhere off the map
was your final service.

Maybe your patience in waiting
for my thoughts to
return to you–gifting me time
for me to be ready, or able,
to miss you–was what I,
a lonely adult, needed.

But now that I am whole,
will you please come back?

Ellie Rose McKee

Beards

I want to write a poem about my beard:
the hairs on my chin, under my moustache;
my lips
                        lopsided in density
                        lilting
to the left.

I want to write a poem about 'beards':
people who are with, or pretend to be with,
queer people to help prevent their Queerness being

        exposed.

I was always worried my beard hid my femininity;
was a mask, hiding the real me,
but under the surface is more surface
and I'm no more feminine at skin level.

(Yes, I said it.)

Does that make me masculine?
Something else? Both?

(Whisper it: *neither?*)

I want to express the complexity of my being;
put it down in verse,
but I can't get the words to rhyme
can't get the… get the… oh, curses!

Now I see why nature plants trees:
to hide the truth.

Linchpins

Slap a sticking plaster on and leave
the body in a valley.

If no one is around to hear,
there is no sound

(but the whispers of hair).

Ellie Rose McKee

A Lesson in Etymology

They talk about giving birth–
about going into labour–
without ever really considering it work.

Look at the birth of this word.
Yes, it is the hardest, most important job.

Yet

who spares a thought for those
constantly failing
the application process?

Linchpins

Homeland

This land I hail from,
this northern land that doesn't even include
the most northerly tip
of the physical earth it shares;
that both is and is not part of
the island it can't escape,

no stone's throw away;
the border as unremarkable as
a gravel driveway fought over
by two old neighbours
with failing faculties and youthful ire
not a single clue between them regarding
what the first grievance was, or when–

this land which is simultaneously part
of another nation, bunched together
as a generalisation; declassified
all the time, and passed over:
ignored. Not important.
Not part of *them*, yet never

                                      alone

never able to exist
on its own axis;

this soil under my feet frustrates me.
My feelings are as mixed up as the history.
How can I hate the whole while loving

each   individual   part?

Ellie Rose McKee

The coast and counties
the dialects and districts
the customs and cultures:
a multi-coloured tradition
with an art palate that comes in more
than two sets of three colours.

This land confuses me
bemuses me
beguiles me

it claims me
and I'm done resisting.

Linchpins

Fragile

The word printed across
the coloured box in bold type, pain-
stakingly centred by hand, and a ruler.

Your most recent unsolicited gift,
complete with an inscription of:
I know you like these.

Complete with carefully chosen
card that matches the colour of
the box and fits just right.

Absent of my given name,
that you never quite cared for;
the whole thing tied up in a

bow and sent, special delivery,
to the daughter you never quite liked
or understood.

I set the box down, my hands furious.
I never liked these – never wanted
any of this.

When the guilt hits, a moment
later, I of course remember
it was supposed to be the gift

all along; the main thing meant
to be dragged out into the present.
You didn't take in care in covering
it at all, and the mailman dented the box.

I'm careful to wash my hands.

Wonder/To Look Up

How big is the sky? A child might ask. An adult might wonder, too, but never voice. Afterall, they can look it up. As though glancing to the sky itself for answers. All the information clinging to the cloud. But they won't do it. They know this even as they put the thought away. It is enough for them to have the *possibility* of knowledge. But I want to know how many stars there are. Want to know if anyone's figured it out yet. Been able to separate the ones that still shine from the ones whose light is only an echo of their past lives. I think the child wonderful for thinking to ask—or to ask without thinking. And think the adult—myself—foolish for not looking to the answer. But then I'd likely stop wondering. And wouldn't that be worse? I look up. Decide it would. Put my phone away.

Linchpins

Bank Holiday Blues

I'm sitting here, in the dark–
candle lit–wondering how
we're gonna make it.

As much in love as ever;
the sad truth creeps–
hides in the dark places:

You can't eat love
for dinner.

Ellie Rose McKee

Bolt

["The electrical energy that powers each cell in our bodies works out at thirty million volts per meter, the equivalent voltage of a bolt of lightning." – The QI Book of Facts]

You are not weak-willed
You are not poorly
You are effervescent
Stardust holds your bones together

Sure, life is hard
But you face it
Things try to hold you down
But you won't be held, forever

You're a firebolt, you are
Light and life flows in your veins
From every action,
And every thought

You are not dull
You are not deficient
In this lonely wasteland,
You're the brightest thing for miles

Linchpins

Diagnosis

Words in the *e t h e r,*

        Symptoms with no name

        THEN a Revelation,

a Title

a Legacy relating Words

        to Conditions;

        the discoverer knitting their Name

        together with the threads,

Labels connected to more personal discoveries,

        connected to Understanding,

        connected to misunderstanding

            and Stigma;

central to the web–

People.

        Lifelines knotted up.

Ellie Rose McKee

Stream of...

Reaching for answers,
I wash dishes twice;
recall the past
an incalculable number of...

times weren't good
there were/are blocks
bl_nk s.

In school, I said,
(I think I said)
My grandmother died
and the other kids understood
but I didn't.

And an eon later, he said that I
need to let go.
I asked how,
but there his answers failed.

He said,
Most people can't remember things
and I said–and am still saying–

No.

Linchpins

The Cost of Words

I counted the number of syllables
on my fingers

The number of pleases and thank-yous
it took to cross the room
on my toes

It's always much more economic
to say I'm fine

Fault Lines

A mentor of mine once noted:
hurt people hurt people.
That is, people who have been hurt
tend to pass it on.
Which does ring true—
does seemed proved,
when matched with experience.

But aren't we all hurt,
and haven't we all been cut?
It makes me question,
how deep one must be
injured, before the urge
to injure wells up.

I'm not sure I want to know
but I do wish I could trace hurt—
      follow it down
           in
                    lines,
    like a family t r e e
        back to its
        roots.

I wish I had the power to
            stop
in motion, that first act—
all the subsequent acts;

I just wish the pain would stop
but I'm not Abel.

Linchpins

Rubatosis

You can claim to be aware
of all that surrounds you
and say that none of that noise escapes, but

But I can tell you the lie of it–
point it right out in your chest.

For how many years
have you had this thundering
right at your very core?

And when was the last time you listened?

Ellie Rose McKee

Paper Hands

You hear about tennis
elbow and swimmer's ear,
but have you ever felt the
hands of a poet?

Touched the dry softness of skin
that's had all its oils absorbed
by journals and notecards,
letters and books–

any available surface that
would give or receive words–
veins showing through papered
skin in which the ink flows?

Acknowledgements

Some of these poems were written during writing workshops with Jen Campbell, who also provided edits on this collection.

A previous version of 'What I Think About When I Can't Sleep' was published by Arlen House in their 2017 'Washing Windows' anthology under the title 'Sounds.'

'Mother Russia' was written for Belfast Writers' Group's third anthology, 'Worlds Within Worlds.'

'Paper Hands' was published online by Nine Muses Poetry in 2019.

www.ingramcontent.com/pod-product-compliance
Lightning Source LLC
Chambersburg PA
CBHW021454080526
44588CB00009B/852